Dibs

Chicago

The Winter Phenomenon of Parking Spot Saving

by Mike Brown
Sandy De Lisle

Dibs Chicago

ISBN: 978-0-9886103-0-9

Book Design by Sandy De Lisle and Mike Brown
Written by Sandy De Lisle and Mike Brown
Cover and Graphic Design by Anne LoCascio
Photography by Laurie Manikowski and Mike Brown

Introduction

If you have ever lived in Chicago, you have undoubtedly heard of the phenomenon known as "DIBS." For the uninitiated, DIBS typically arrives in Chicago just in time for the winter holidays. And during this season of peace and goodwill, it brings its own little "Miracle on 34th Street" (and Leavitt, and Argyle, and Lawrence and . . .).

You see, DIBS is a time-"honored" tradition in Chicago (and other snowy cities like Philadelphia, Minneapolis and Boston) whereby a person who shovels out a public street parking space is entitled to that space, theoretically until the spring thaw. And, as is showcased in this book, in order to secure the space, a variety of objects such as chairs, milk crates, ironing boards or plastic penguins can be used as space savers. From 2008 to 2012 our team photographed DIBS placeholders from Austin to Lakeview and Humboldt Park to Wrigleyville. Only the most telling—and entertaining—were selected for this book.

In its worst form, "unethical DIBSters" simply remove their street-parked car after a snowstorm, without any shoveling or physical exertion, and place an item in the spot where their car was parked. This is akin to "finishing" the Chicago Marathon by joining the race at the 25-Mile Marker. After all, according to some, there is a DIBS code of conduct, some physical exertion and sweating for your space is required.

So how did DIBS become a household word in Chicago? Some attribute it to *Chicago Tribune* writer John Kass—one of its biggest defenders—who has frequently written about DIBS in his column.

Others say former Chicago Mayor Richard M. Daley made it popular by unofficially sanctioning it, "If someone spends all their time digging their car out, do not drive into that spot. This is Chicago. Fair warning."

In 2010, toward the end of Mayor Daley's 22-year reign over Chicago, a group called Chair-Free Chicago set out to undo DIBS, asking people to forego what in their eyes is an unneighborly practice. The group encourages Chicagoans to post Chair-Free zone signs on trees and buildings where DIBSing occurs. They also suggest that neighbors come together and collectively shovel the entire street, rather than just one space.

But since this *is* Chicago, some community-building anti-DIBSsters are more forceful in their disdain for the practice. In the words of one Chicagoan who posted on Chair-Free Chicago's website, "Get your crap off the street."

Whether you believe DIBS is more "Miracle on 34th Street" or "Ebenezer Scrooge," we invite you to spend some time observing DIBS in Chicago this winter. And to make your DIBS viewing more enjoyable, we have provided a handy checklist for you to use at the end of the book. Make sure to send us your best DIBS photos for publication on our website and future editions of this book. Email us at submit@dibschicago.com.

Enjoy the Winter Season!
Mike Brown, Sandy De Lisle and Laurie Manikowski

We hope you enjoy our photo selections!

Chapter 1— Most Popular

Some items, like chairs and milk crates, are synonymous with DIBS. Perhaps, in the case of chairs, it is because they are so readily available—and provide a handy place to sit and rest while you are shoveling out YOUR space. Even though chairs are the most frequently used placeholders (and the symbol of the anti-DIBS movement), it's the variety of chairs used and their placement that keep them from being boring. From upholstered chairs to lawn chairs to stools, the sheer diversity of seating provides the DIBS watcher hours of entertainment. And when you factor in the strategic—and sometimes artistic— placement of the chairs, DIBS viewing becomes more interesting than the traditional "driving around and looking at people's Christmas lights."

The ubiquitous milk crate begins to appear in city streets just in time for the first snowfall. To the unknowing observer, it may appear as if Chicagoans have jumped on board the locavore movement and are having their milk delivered like in the olden days. Alas, they would be wrong. The milk crate, according to our scientifically unproven study, is second only to the chair in frequency of use. Again, the reasons for its popularity may be similar to that of the chair: it is a common household item, provides a place to rest your weary body whilst shoveling, and it has the added advantage of being extremely portable, lightweight, stackable and cheap.

The Chicago Classic

Daley Dibs
Well, he is retired now . . .

"I'll Take One of Each."

Formal Seating

Gone . . .

South

"Flip Off!"

Gone . . . Fishin'

Retro Dibs

Last Legs

"Gather Round Youngins."

"Hi, Chair!"

Table for One

Stool Sample

Ringside

"I Mean Business!"

"All In."

The Dispute

"And the Broom Does What Now!??"

Crate Training

Catch of the Day

Occupied

"Got Milk?"

Chapter 2—Most Trashy

Whereas chairs, cribs, and barbeques can look whimsical—and borderline festive—lining Chicago's streets, even the biggest DIBS advocate would agree that some placeholders are low class and, well, trashy. Using garbage, garbage cans and unidentifiable junk is not only unsightly, it makes it difficult for a DIBS watcher to distinguish what it is they have sighted. If the City of Chicago ever does decide to start enforcing the City's littering and dumping ordinances, and outlaw DIBS, it will do so because of the DIBS practitioners whose choice in placeholders make it look like Streets and Sanitation workers are on vacation.

Everything
But the Kitchen Sink

Yard Sale

Boxing Day

"Move Along . . .
No Parking Here!"

Covering All the Bases

The Bucket Boys-On Break

Jugs

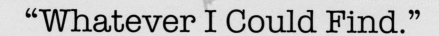

"Whatever I Could Find."

Chapter 3—Most Artistic

Lest you get the impression that DIBSing is practiced by brutish individuals with no sense of aesthetics, rest assured that many DIBSters have an artistic flair that is evidenced in their placeholders. Indeed some of their space savers resemble sculptures or avant-garde architecture. Perhaps, one could argue, DIBS adds to the cultural and artistic vibe of the city. After all, our first example reminds us of a certain famous artist's sculpture in Daley Plaza…

Street Picasso

Balancing Acts

"Walk the Plank!"

Evil Kneivel

"Top That!"

Chapter 4—
Most Creative

To further the argument that DIBS may be adding to the cultural and artistic fiber of the city of Chicago, there's no doubt that DIBSing challenges residents to come up with ways to use ordinary—and not so ordinary—objects in their placeholder creations. In some sense, it also promotes the City's commitment to recycling in that it encourages the repurposing of unused items.

This Won't be Here Long.

Sleeping Around

Best Use of a Phone Book

On Loan
from Lincoln Park Zoo

Proof that MSG Causes Headaches

"Now Clean It Up!"

Chapter 5—Most Official

Since DIBS almost seems official when you consider how it promotes the arts, creativity and recycling, it's only fitting that some practitioners choose to use official looking items like flags, cones and City traffic horses to cordon off their newly acquired parking space. To hold the view that DIBS really is official, we just have to ignore the City ordinances on littering and dumping, but, hey, if the former mayor can do that . . .

DIBS: Number One Reason
for Puerto Rico
to join the Union

City Employee?

"It's Soooooo Official."

"I'm Not Horsin' Around!"

Caution

Laying Down on the Job

"Really???!!!"

Chapter 6—Most Childish

Although many children's items are used as placeholders in DIBS, do not be fooled into thinking DIBSing is child's play. There have been many incidents where fights have broken out over someone "stealing" another person's space that was marked with a Big Wheel or Dora the Explorer© bean bag chair. And if you think about it, the folks who use children's items as placeholders are perhaps the craftiest of all, because who but the Grinchiest or reckless is going to move a children's toy or throw caution to the wind and park in a space where an abandoned baby stroller might mean there is a loose baby nearby who just might slip under your tires.

"Oh, Pooh!"

Reserved for Tony Hawke

"No, Mommy, That's My Toy!"

"Everyone Contributes in This Family!"

The Cradle Will Fall.

DIBS-in-Training

"Get Out and Walk!"

"Aye Caramba!"

Everything a Spider Can . . .

Chapter 7—Most Busted

Since DIBS is technically illegal, catching a DIBSter in the act, can be difficult. And as the anti-DIBS movement gains hold, these sightings may become even more uncommon. In the photos that follow, we capture a rare glimpse of DIBSing as it is taking place. We have blurred the image of the perpetrator to protect the DIBSter from prosecution.

Don't be fooled by the appearance of this DIBSter.
She may seem nonchalant, but if you try
to park in her space, you may end up with
a chair in your windshield.

Chapter 8—
Most Polite...Or Not

DIBS brings out strong emotions in people. Those in favor of DIBS believe that if they have taken the time and expended the heart attack inducing exertion it takes to shovel out a street parking space—even on public property—they have the right to that space. And since Streets and Sanitation can be less than prompt after a big snowfall, that mentality is somewhat understandable. Diehard DIBSters believe that as long as they maintain "their" space after each snowfall, it is "theirs" until spring. Other DIBSters feel they only have rights to the space until the next major snowfall. After that, whoever clears the space first can then stake his or her claim (or, as the case may be, chair) on the space.

Opponents of DIBS believe that not only is DIBS illegal, since it violates City ordinances, it is a violation of community spirit, pitting neighbor against neighbor. And in a season of peace and goodwill, DIBSing can be particularly hard to stomach—especially when accompanied with egg nog.

What is interesting to observe—and is captured on the next pages is what happens when DIBsters and non-DIBSters collide . . .

Naughty or Nice?

In these photos we see a polite note, presumably
left by a DIBSter, asking neighbors to refrain
from taking "their" parking space. You will
notice that the person who wrote the note did
not curse or escalate matters. He or she (OK,
with the prominent smiley face decoration, let's
just say "she") simply asked would-be parkers
to look elsewhere.

In this photo taken in the same neighborhood, a different and perhaps angrier DIBSter leaves a non-smiley face adorned note. We presume that a neighbor and non-DIBSter had accused them of not exerting the necessary physical effort of shoveling before "reserving" the space. This sign is a response to that insinuation, making it clear in the Queen's English that the DIBSter has now properly shoveled the space, and thus now has all DIBS rights to it.... further challenging anyone to prove otherwise.

Chapter 9-
DIBS-Watching Checklist

To make your DIBS-watching more enjoyable, we have included a handy checklist in order for you to keep track of your sightings.

Readers' Official DIBS Checklist

CHAIRS

 ___ Wooden chair

 ___ Lawn Chair

 ___ Formal Dining Chair

 ___ Retro Vinyl and Metal chair

 ___ Rocking Chair

 ___ Stool

 ___ Other

MILK CRATES

 ___ Black

 ___ White
(Careful these can be well-camouflaged in the snow)

 ___ Red

 ___ Green

___Other Color

MISCELLANEOUS HOUSEHOLD ITEMS

 ___ Bed frame

 ___ Table

 ___ Barbeque Grill

 ___ Speaker

 ___ Other

CHILDREN'S ITEMS

 ___ Bike

 ___ Stroller

 ___ Dora the Explorer© Object
(or any other beloved children's character)

 ___ Crib/Playpen

 ___ Skateboard

 ___ Other

"OFFICIAL" ITEMS

 ___ Cones

 ___ Horses

 ___ Flags

OTHER

___ No-Chair Zone Poster

___ Mayor Richard M. Daley

___ John Kass

 ___ Someone Caught in the Act of DIBSing

References

About us. (2010). Retrieved from http://www.chairfreechicago.org/about.php

Adams, C. (2011, February 3). How did parking-spot "dibs" start in Chicago, and what are the rules. Straight Dope Chicago. Retrieved from http://chicago.straightdope.com/sdc20110203.php

Kass, J. (2012, January 13). John kass becomes judge dibs, ruling dibs junk is chicago street art. Chicago Tribune. Retrieved from http://articles.chicagotribune.com/2012-01-13/news/ct-met-kass-0113-20120113_1_judge-dibs-dibstitution-shovel

Zorn, E. (2005, December 15). No one seems to have dibs on word's origins. Chicago Tribune. Retrieved from http://blogs.chicagotribune.com/news_columnists_ezorn/2005/12/no_one_seems_to.html

To order more copies of DIBS: Chicago,
please visit www.dibschicago.com